50 Keto-Friendly Dinner Recipes

By: Kelly Johnson

Table of Contents

- Garlic Butter Steak with Roasted Vegetables
- Creamy Tuscan Chicken
- Bacon-Wrapped Chicken Thighs
- Keto Cheeseburger Casserole
- Lemon Garlic Butter Salmon
- Zucchini Noodles with Pesto and Shrimp
- Buffalo Chicken Stuffed Peppers
- Keto Beef Stroganoff
- Cauliflower Crust Pizza
- Sausage and Cabbage Skillet
- Spaghetti Squash Carbonara
- Pork Chops with Garlic Herb Butter
- Chicken Alfredo with Zucchini Noodles
- Avocado Egg Salad Lettuce Wraps
- Garlic Parmesan Brussels Sprouts with Bacon
- Shrimp Scampi with Zucchini Noodles
- Keto Chili (No Beans)
- Cheesy Broccoli and Chicken Casserole
- Eggplant Parmesan (Keto Version)
- Stuffed Portobello Mushrooms
- Baked Salmon with Dill Sauce
- Keto Meatloaf with Almond Flour
- Cabbage and Ground Beef Stir-Fry
- Keto Tacos with Cheese Shells
- Asian-Style Cauliflower Fried Rice
- Pesto Chicken with Roasted Asparagus
- Bacon and Egg Cauliflower Fried Rice
- Creamy Garlic Shrimp with Spinach
- Keto BBQ Ribs
- Low-Carb Beef and Broccoli Stir-Fry
- Keto Shepherd's Pie with Cauliflower Mash
- Jalapeño Popper Chicken Casserole
- Grilled Lamb Chops with Herb Butter
- Keto Cobb Salad with Ranch Dressing
- Keto Philly Cheesesteak Skillet

- Roasted Garlic and Herb Butter Pork Tenderloin
- Keto-Friendly Shrimp Tacos with Cabbage Slaw
- Crack Chicken (Creamy Ranch Bacon Chicken)
- Keto Egg Roll in a Bowl
- Low-Carb Chicken Parmesan
- Keto-Friendly Gumbo
- Baked Feta and Tomato Zoodles
- Stuffed Chicken Breast with Cream Cheese and Spinach
- Keto Tuna Melt on Cloud Bread
- Garlic Butter Baked Cod
- Keto Greek Meatballs with Tzatziki Sauce
- Keto Fried Chicken (Almond Flour Breading)
- Keto Zuppa Toscana Soup
- Keto Bacon-Wrapped Meatballs
- Spinach and Cheese Stuffed Mushrooms

Garlic Butter Steak with Roasted Vegetables

Ingredients:

- 2 ribeye or sirloin steaks
- 2 tbsp butter
- 3 cloves garlic, minced
- 1 tsp fresh thyme
- 1 tsp salt
- ½ tsp black pepper
- 1 cup broccoli florets
- 1 cup bell peppers, sliced
- 1 tbsp olive oil

Instructions:

1. **Preheat Oven:** Set to 400°F (200°C).
2. **Roast Vegetables:** Toss vegetables with olive oil, salt, and pepper. Roast for 20 minutes.
3. **Cook Steak:** Heat a skillet over high heat, sear steaks for 3 minutes per side.
4. **Add Garlic Butter:** Lower heat, add butter, garlic, and thyme. Spoon butter over steaks.
5. **Serve:** Rest steak for 5 minutes before slicing. Serve with roasted vegetables.

Creamy Tuscan Chicken

Ingredients:

- 2 boneless, skinless chicken breasts
- 2 tbsp butter
- 3 cloves garlic, minced
- ½ cup sun-dried tomatoes, chopped
- 1 cup heavy cream
- ½ cup grated Parmesan cheese
- 1 cup spinach
- 1 tsp Italian seasoning
- Salt and pepper to taste

Instructions:

1. **Cook Chicken:** Season and sear in butter until golden. Set aside.
2. **Make Sauce:** Sauté garlic, add sun-dried tomatoes, heavy cream, Parmesan, and Italian seasoning.
3. **Combine:** Return chicken to skillet, add spinach, and simmer until sauce thickens.
4. **Serve:** Enjoy over zucchini noodles or cauliflower rice.

Bacon-Wrapped Chicken Thighs

Ingredients:

- 4 boneless, skinless chicken thighs
- 4 slices bacon
- 1 tsp garlic powder
- 1 tsp smoked paprika
- Salt and pepper to taste

Instructions:

1. **Preheat Oven:** Set to 375°F (190°C).
2. **Season Chicken:** Sprinkle chicken thighs with garlic powder, paprika, salt, and pepper.
3. **Wrap with Bacon:** Wrap each thigh with a slice of bacon.
4. **Bake:** Place on a baking sheet and bake for 25-30 minutes.
5. **Serve:** Enjoy with roasted vegetables or salad.

Keto Cheeseburger Casserole

Ingredients:

- 1 lb ground beef
- ½ cup chopped onions
- 1 cup shredded cheddar cheese
- 3 eggs
- ½ cup heavy cream
- 1 tsp mustard
- ½ tsp salt
- ½ tsp black pepper

Instructions:

1. **Preheat Oven:** Set to 375°F (190°C).
2. **Cook Beef:** Brown ground beef with onions, drain excess fat.
3. **Mix & Bake:** Combine eggs, cream, mustard, salt, and pepper. Layer beef in a baking dish, pour egg mixture over, top with cheese.
4. **Bake:** Cook for 25 minutes until cheese is melted.

Lemon Garlic Butter Salmon

Ingredients:

- 2 salmon fillets
- 2 tbsp butter
- 2 cloves garlic, minced
- 1 tbsp lemon juice
- 1 tsp fresh parsley
- Salt and pepper to taste

Instructions:

1. **Preheat Oven:** Set to 400°F (200°C).
2. **Make Butter Mixture:** Mix butter, garlic, lemon juice, and parsley.
3. **Bake Salmon:** Place salmon on a baking sheet, spread butter mixture on top, and bake for 12-15 minutes.
4. **Serve:** Enjoy with roasted asparagus or cauliflower mash.

Zucchini Noodles with Pesto and Shrimp

Ingredients:

- 2 zucchinis, spiralized
- 1 cup cooked shrimp
- 2 tbsp pesto
- 1 tbsp olive oil
- ½ tsp salt
- ¼ tsp black pepper

Instructions:

1. **Sauté Shrimp:** Heat olive oil in a pan and cook shrimp for 2 minutes per side.
2. **Toss with Zoodles:** Add zucchini noodles and pesto, toss until coated.
3. **Serve:** Enjoy with grated Parmesan cheese.

Buffalo Chicken Stuffed Peppers

Ingredients:

- 2 bell peppers, halved
- 1 cup shredded cooked chicken
- ¼ cup buffalo sauce
- ½ cup shredded cheese
- 2 tbsp ranch dressing

Instructions:

1. **Preheat Oven:** Set to 375°F (190°C).
2. **Mix Filling:** Combine chicken, buffalo sauce, and ranch dressing.
3. **Stuff Peppers:** Fill pepper halves with the mixture, top with cheese.
4. **Bake:** Cook for 20 minutes until cheese is bubbly.

Keto Beef Stroganoff

Ingredients:

- 1 lb beef sirloin, sliced
- 1 cup mushrooms, sliced
- 1 cup heavy cream
- ½ cup beef broth
- 1 tbsp Dijon mustard
- 2 cloves garlic, minced
- 2 tbsp butter

Instructions:

1. **Sear Beef:** Cook beef in butter until browned, then set aside.
2. **Sauté Mushrooms & Garlic:** Add mushrooms and garlic to the pan.
3. **Make Sauce:** Stir in broth, heavy cream, and mustard. Simmer until thick.
4. **Combine & Serve:** Return beef to pan and serve over cauliflower rice or zucchini noodles.

Cauliflower Crust Pizza

Ingredients:

- 2 cups cauliflower rice
- 1 egg
- ½ cup shredded mozzarella cheese
- ½ tsp Italian seasoning
- ¼ tsp salt
- **Toppings:** Tomato sauce, cheese, pepperoni, vegetables

Instructions:

1. **Preheat Oven:** Set to 400°F (200°C).
2. **Make Crust:** Microwave cauliflower rice for 5 minutes, then squeeze out moisture. Mix with egg, cheese, seasoning, and salt.
3. **Bake:** Form into a crust on a baking sheet and bake for 15 minutes.
4. **Add Toppings:** Spread sauce, add cheese and toppings, then bake for 10 more minutes.

Sausage and Cabbage Skillet

Ingredients:

- 1 lb smoked sausage, sliced
- ½ head cabbage, chopped
- 1 small onion, sliced
- 2 cloves garlic, minced
- 1 tbsp olive oil
- ½ tsp salt
- ¼ tsp black pepper
- ½ tsp smoked paprika

Instructions:

1. **Sauté Sausage:** Heat oil in a skillet and cook sausage until browned.
2. **Add Vegetables:** Stir in onions, garlic, and cabbage.
3. **Season & Cook:** Add salt, pepper, and paprika. Cook for 10 minutes until cabbage is tender.
4. **Serve:** Enjoy warm with mustard or hot sauce.

Spaghetti Squash Carbonara

Ingredients:

- 1 medium spaghetti squash
- 4 slices bacon, chopped
- 2 eggs
- ½ cup grated Parmesan cheese
- 2 cloves garlic, minced
- ½ tsp black pepper
- 1 tbsp butter

Instructions:

1. **Prepare Squash:** Cut spaghetti squash in half, remove seeds, and bake at 400°F (200°C) for 40 minutes.
2. **Cook Bacon & Garlic:** Sauté bacon until crispy, then add garlic.
3. **Mix Eggs & Cheese:** Whisk eggs and Parmesan together.
4. **Assemble Dish:** Scrape spaghetti squash strands into a bowl, toss with butter, bacon, and garlic.
5. **Add Sauce:** Mix in egg mixture quickly to create a creamy sauce.

Pork Chops with Garlic Herb Butter

Ingredients:

- 2 pork chops
- 2 tbsp butter
- 2 cloves garlic, minced
- 1 tsp fresh thyme
- ½ tsp salt
- ¼ tsp black pepper

Instructions:

1. **Sear Pork Chops:** Heat a skillet and cook pork chops for 4 minutes per side.
2. **Add Butter & Herbs:** Reduce heat, add butter, garlic, and thyme. Spoon butter over chops.
3. **Rest & Serve:** Let rest for 5 minutes before serving.

Chicken Alfredo with Zucchini Noodles

Ingredients:

- 2 chicken breasts, sliced
- 2 zucchinis, spiralized
- 1 cup heavy cream
- ½ cup grated Parmesan cheese
- 2 cloves garlic, minced
- 1 tbsp butter
- Salt and pepper to taste

Instructions:

1. **Cook Chicken:** Sauté chicken in butter until golden.
2. **Make Alfredo Sauce:** Stir in garlic, heavy cream, and Parmesan. Simmer until thickened.
3. **Toss with Zoodles:** Add zucchini noodles and cook for 1-2 minutes.
4. **Serve:** Enjoy warm with extra Parmesan.

Avocado Egg Salad Lettuce Wraps

Ingredients:

- 2 hard-boiled eggs, chopped
- 1 avocado, mashed
- 1 tbsp mayonnaise
- 1 tsp lemon juice
- ½ tsp salt
- ¼ tsp black pepper
- 4 large lettuce leaves

Instructions:

1. **Make Egg Salad:** Mix eggs, avocado, mayo, lemon juice, salt, and pepper.
2. **Assemble Wraps:** Spoon into lettuce leaves and wrap.
3. **Serve:** Enjoy fresh.

Garlic Parmesan Brussels Sprouts with Bacon

Ingredients:

- 1 lb Brussels sprouts, halved
- 4 slices bacon, chopped
- 2 cloves garlic, minced
- ½ cup grated Parmesan cheese
- 1 tbsp olive oil
- Salt and pepper to taste

Instructions:

1. **Preheat Oven:** Set to 400°F (200°C).
2. **Roast Brussels Sprouts:** Toss with olive oil, salt, and pepper. Bake for 20 minutes.
3. **Cook Bacon & Garlic:** Sauté bacon until crispy, add garlic.
4. **Combine & Serve:** Toss Brussels sprouts with bacon and Parmesan.

Shrimp Scampi with Zucchini Noodles

Ingredients:

- 1 lb shrimp, peeled and deveined
- 2 zucchinis, spiralized
- 2 tbsp butter
- 2 cloves garlic, minced
- ½ cup chicken broth
- 1 tbsp lemon juice
- ½ tsp red pepper flakes
- Salt and pepper to taste

Instructions:

1. **Sauté Garlic & Shrimp:** Melt butter, cook shrimp until pink.
2. **Make Sauce:** Add garlic, broth, lemon juice, and red pepper flakes. Simmer for 2 minutes.
3. **Toss with Zoodles:** Add zucchini noodles and cook for 1-2 minutes.
4. **Serve:** Enjoy warm with extra lemon juice.

Keto Chili (No Beans)

Ingredients:

- 1 lb ground beef
- ½ onion, chopped
- 2 cloves garlic, minced
- 1 cup diced tomatoes
- 1 cup beef broth
- 1 tsp chili powder
- ½ tsp cumin
- ½ tsp paprika
- Salt and pepper to taste

Instructions:

1. **Cook Beef & Onions:** Brown ground beef with onions and garlic.
2. **Add Seasonings:** Stir in tomatoes, broth, and spices.
3. **Simmer:** Cook on low heat for 20 minutes.
4. **Serve:** Enjoy with shredded cheese and sour cream.

Cheesy Broccoli and Chicken Casserole

Ingredients:

- 2 cups cooked chicken, shredded
- 2 cups broccoli florets
- 1 cup shredded cheddar cheese
- ½ cup heavy cream
- 2 tbsp cream cheese
- 1 tsp garlic powder
- ½ tsp salt
- ¼ tsp black pepper

Instructions:

1. **Preheat Oven:** Set to 375°F (190°C).
2. **Make Sauce:** Heat cream cheese, heavy cream, and garlic powder.
3. **Assemble Casserole:** Combine chicken, broccoli, and sauce in a baking dish.
4. **Bake:** Sprinkle with cheese and bake for 20 minutes.

Eggplant Parmesan (Keto Version)

Ingredients:

- 1 large eggplant, sliced
- 1 cup almond flour
- ½ cup grated Parmesan cheese
- 1 egg, beaten
- 1 cup sugar-free marinara sauce
- 1 cup shredded mozzarella cheese
- 1 tsp Italian seasoning
- Salt and pepper to taste

Instructions:

1. **Preheat Oven:** Set to 375°F (190°C).
2. **Prepare Eggplant:** Sprinkle salt on slices, let sit for 10 minutes, then pat dry.
3. **Bread & Bake:** Dip eggplant in egg, then coat with almond flour and Parmesan. Bake for 20 minutes.
4. **Assemble & Bake Again:** Layer baked eggplant with marinara sauce and mozzarella. Bake for another 15 minutes until bubbly.

Stuffed Portobello Mushrooms

Ingredients:

- 4 large Portobello mushrooms
- 1 cup cooked ground beef or sausage
- ½ cup cream cheese
- ½ cup shredded mozzarella
- 1 tsp garlic powder
- ½ tsp salt
- ½ tsp black pepper

Instructions:

1. **Preheat Oven:** Set to 375°F (190°C).
2. **Prepare Mushrooms:** Remove stems and place caps on a baking sheet.
3. **Make Filling:** Mix cooked beef/sausage with cream cheese, mozzarella, garlic powder, salt, and pepper.
4. **Stuff & Bake:** Fill mushrooms and bake for 15-20 minutes.

Baked Salmon with Dill Sauce

Ingredients:

- 2 salmon fillets
- 2 tbsp butter
- 1 tbsp fresh dill, chopped
- 1 tbsp lemon juice
- 2 cloves garlic, minced
- ½ cup sour cream

Instructions:

1. **Preheat Oven:** Set to 400°F (200°C).
2. **Bake Salmon:** Place salmon on a baking sheet, season with salt and pepper, and bake for 12-15 minutes.
3. **Make Sauce:** Mix sour cream, dill, lemon juice, garlic, salt, and pepper.
4. **Serve:** Spoon sauce over salmon.

Keto Meatloaf with Almond Flour

Ingredients:

- 1 lb ground beef
- ½ cup almond flour
- 1 egg
- ½ cup shredded cheese
- 1 tsp garlic powder
- 1 tsp onion powder
- 1 tsp salt
- ½ tsp black pepper
- ½ cup sugar-free ketchup

Instructions:

1. **Preheat Oven:** Set to 375°F (190°C).
2. **Mix Ingredients:** Combine all ingredients except ketchup.
3. **Shape & Bake:** Form into a loaf on a baking sheet and bake for 30 minutes.
4. **Add Topping & Bake Again:** Spread ketchup on top and bake for 10 more minutes.

Cabbage and Ground Beef Stir-Fry

Ingredients:

- 1 lb ground beef
- ½ head cabbage, shredded
- 1 small onion, chopped
- 2 cloves garlic, minced
- 2 tbsp soy sauce or coconut aminos
- 1 tsp sesame oil
- ½ tsp red pepper flakes

Instructions:

1. **Cook Beef:** Brown ground beef in a pan, then set aside.
2. **Sauté Vegetables:** Cook onion, garlic, and cabbage until softened.
3. **Combine & Season:** Return beef to pan, add soy sauce, sesame oil, and red pepper flakes.

Keto Tacos with Cheese Shells

Ingredients:

- 1 cup shredded cheddar cheese
- ½ lb ground beef
- ½ tsp cumin
- ½ tsp chili powder
- ¼ tsp garlic powder
- ¼ tsp salt
- ½ avocado, sliced
- ¼ cup sour cream

Instructions:

1. **Make Cheese Shells:** Bake small piles of shredded cheese at 375°F (190°C) for 7-10 minutes until golden. Let cool over a wooden spoon to form a taco shape.
2. **Cook Beef:** Brown beef with seasonings.
3. **Assemble Tacos:** Fill cheese shells with beef, avocado, and sour cream.

Asian-Style Cauliflower Fried Rice

Ingredients:

- 2 cups riced cauliflower
- 1 egg, beaten
- ½ cup diced chicken or shrimp
- 2 tbsp soy sauce or coconut aminos
- 1 tsp sesame oil
- 2 cloves garlic, minced
- ¼ cup green onions, chopped

Instructions:

1. **Sauté Garlic & Protein:** Cook garlic and chicken/shrimp in a pan.
2. **Cook Cauliflower Rice:** Add cauliflower and stir-fry for 5 minutes.
3. **Scramble Egg:** Push rice aside, pour in egg, and scramble.
4. **Season & Serve:** Mix everything together, add soy sauce and sesame oil, and top with green onions.

Pesto Chicken with Roasted Asparagus

Ingredients:

- 2 chicken breasts
- 2 tbsp pesto
- 1 cup asparagus spears
- 1 tbsp olive oil
- Salt and pepper to taste

Instructions:

1. **Preheat Oven:** Set to 375°F (190°C).
2. **Prepare Chicken:** Coat chicken breasts with pesto.
3. **Roast Asparagus:** Toss asparagus with olive oil, salt, and pepper.
4. **Bake:** Place chicken and asparagus on a baking sheet and bake for 25 minutes.

Bacon and Egg Cauliflower Fried Rice

Ingredients:

- 2 cups riced cauliflower
- 2 slices bacon, chopped
- 2 eggs
- 2 cloves garlic, minced
- 2 tbsp soy sauce or coconut aminos
- 1 tsp sesame oil
- ¼ cup green onions, chopped

Instructions:

1. **Cook Bacon:** Sauté bacon until crispy, then set aside.
2. **Sauté Garlic & Cauliflower:** Cook garlic and cauliflower rice in bacon fat for 5 minutes.
3. **Scramble Eggs:** Push rice aside, pour in eggs, and scramble.
4. **Mix & Serve:** Stir in soy sauce, sesame oil, and bacon. Top with green onions.

Creamy Garlic Shrimp with Spinach

Ingredients:

- 1 lb shrimp, peeled and deveined
- 2 tbsp butter
- 3 cloves garlic, minced
- 1 cup heavy cream
- ½ cup grated Parmesan cheese
- 2 cups fresh spinach
- ½ tsp salt
- ¼ tsp black pepper
- 1 tsp lemon juice

Instructions:

1. **Cook Shrimp:** Heat butter in a pan and sauté shrimp for 2 minutes per side. Remove and set aside.
2. **Make Sauce:** Sauté garlic, then add heavy cream, Parmesan, salt, and pepper. Simmer until thick.
3. **Add Spinach & Shrimp:** Stir in spinach until wilted, then return shrimp to the pan.
4. **Serve:** Drizzle with lemon juice and enjoy!

Keto BBQ Ribs

Ingredients:

- 2 lbs pork ribs
- 1 tbsp smoked paprika
- 1 tsp garlic powder
- 1 tsp salt
- ½ tsp black pepper
- 1 cup sugar-free BBQ sauce

Instructions:

1. **Preheat Oven:** Set to 300°F (150°C).
2. **Season Ribs:** Rub ribs with paprika, garlic powder, salt, and pepper.
3. **Bake Covered:** Wrap ribs in foil and bake for 2.5 hours.
4. **Glaze & Broil:** Brush with BBQ sauce and broil for 5 minutes until caramelized.

Low-Carb Beef and Broccoli Stir-Fry

Ingredients:

- 1 lb beef sirloin, thinly sliced
- 2 cups broccoli florets
- 2 tbsp soy sauce or coconut aminos
- 1 tbsp sesame oil
- 2 cloves garlic, minced
- ½ tsp ginger, grated
- ½ tsp red pepper flakes

Instructions:

1. **Cook Beef:** Sauté beef in sesame oil until browned, then set aside.
2. **Sauté Broccoli & Aromatics:** Stir-fry garlic, ginger, and broccoli.
3. **Combine & Serve:** Add beef back to the pan, stir in soy sauce, and cook for 2 minutes.

Keto Shepherd's Pie with Cauliflower Mash

Ingredients:

- **Filling:**
    - 1 lb ground beef or lamb
    - ½ onion, chopped
    - 2 cloves garlic, minced
    - ½ cup diced carrots
    - ½ cup beef broth
    - 1 tsp Worcestershire sauce
    - ½ tsp salt
- **Cauliflower Mash:**
    - 2 cups cauliflower florets
    - 2 tbsp butter
    - ¼ cup heavy cream
    - ½ cup shredded cheese

Instructions:

1. **Cook Filling:** Sauté onion, garlic, carrots, and ground beef. Add broth and Worcestershire sauce. Simmer until thickened.
2. **Make Cauliflower Mash:** Steam cauliflower, then blend with butter, cream, and cheese.
3. **Assemble & Bake:** Spread cauliflower mash over meat mixture in a baking dish and bake at 375°F (190°C) for 20 minutes.

Jalapeño Popper Chicken Casserole

Ingredients:

- 2 cups shredded cooked chicken
- 4 slices bacon, chopped
- ½ cup cream cheese
- ½ cup shredded cheddar cheese
- 2 jalapeños, sliced
- ½ tsp garlic powder

Instructions:

1. **Preheat Oven:** Set to 375°F (190°C).
2. **Mix Filling:** Combine chicken, cream cheese, cheddar, bacon, and garlic powder.
3. **Assemble & Bake:** Spread in a baking dish, top with jalapeño slices, and bake for 20 minutes.

Grilled Lamb Chops with Herb Butter

Ingredients:

- 4 lamb chops
- 2 tbsp olive oil
- 1 tsp garlic powder
- 1 tsp rosemary, chopped
- ½ tsp salt
- ¼ tsp black pepper
- 2 tbsp butter

Instructions:

1. **Season Lamb:** Rub lamb chops with olive oil, garlic powder, rosemary, salt, and pepper.
2. **Grill:** Cook on medium-high heat for 3-4 minutes per side.
3. **Add Herb Butter:** Melt butter over hot chops and serve.

Keto Cobb Salad with Ranch Dressing

Ingredients:

- 2 cups romaine lettuce, chopped
- 1 grilled chicken breast, sliced
- 2 boiled eggs, chopped
- 4 slices bacon, crumbled
- ½ avocado, diced
- ½ cup cherry tomatoes, halved
- ¼ cup blue cheese crumbles
- **Dressing:** ¼ cup mayonnaise, 2 tbsp sour cream, 1 tsp garlic powder, 1 tbsp lemon juice, salt & pepper

Instructions:

1. **Assemble Salad:** Arrange lettuce, chicken, eggs, bacon, avocado, tomatoes, and cheese.
2. **Make Dressing:** Whisk all dressing ingredients together.
3. **Serve:** Drizzle with ranch dressing.

Keto Philly Cheesesteak Skillet

Ingredients:

- 1 lb sirloin steak, thinly sliced
- ½ bell pepper, sliced
- ½ onion, sliced
- 1 cup mushrooms, sliced
- 2 tbsp butter
- ½ tsp salt
- ½ tsp black pepper
- ½ cup shredded provolone cheese

Instructions:

1. **Sauté Vegetables:** Cook onions, peppers, and mushrooms in butter.
2. **Cook Steak:** Add steak, salt, and pepper, cooking until browned.
3. **Melt Cheese:** Top with provolone, cover, and let melt.

Roasted Garlic and Herb Butter Pork Tenderloin

Ingredients:

- 1 pork tenderloin
- 2 tbsp butter, softened
- 2 cloves garlic, minced
- 1 tsp rosemary, chopped
- 1 tsp thyme, chopped
- ½ tsp salt
- ¼ tsp black pepper

Instructions:

1. **Preheat Oven:** Set to 400°F (200°C).
2. **Season Pork:** Rub with butter, garlic, herbs, salt, and pepper.
3. **Sear & Roast:** Sear in a hot pan for 2 minutes per side, then bake for 20 minutes.
4. **Rest & Serve:** Let rest for 5 minutes before slicing.

Keto-Friendly Shrimp Tacos with Cabbage Slaw

Ingredients:

- **For the shrimp:**
    - 1 lb shrimp, peeled and deveined
    - 1 tbsp olive oil
    - 1 tsp chili powder
    - ½ tsp garlic powder
    - ½ tsp cumin
    - Salt and pepper to taste
- **For the slaw:**
    - 2 cups shredded cabbage
    - 2 tbsp mayonnaise
    - 1 tbsp lime juice
    - ½ tsp salt
- **For the taco shells:**
    - 1 cup shredded cheddar cheese

Instructions:

1. **Make Cheese Shells:** Place small piles of shredded cheese on a baking sheet and bake at 375°F (190°C) for 7-10 minutes until golden. Let cool slightly, then shape into taco shells.
2. **Cook Shrimp:** Heat oil in a skillet, cook shrimp with seasonings for 3 minutes per side.
3. **Make Slaw:** Mix cabbage, mayo, lime juice, and salt.
4. **Assemble Tacos:** Fill cheese shells with slaw and shrimp.

Crack Chicken (Creamy Ranch Bacon Chicken)

Ingredients:

- 2 boneless, skinless chicken breasts
- ½ cup cream cheese
- ½ cup shredded cheddar cheese
- 4 slices bacon, cooked and crumbled
- 1 tbsp ranch seasoning
- ½ tsp garlic powder
- ½ tsp black pepper

Instructions:

1. **Preheat Oven:** Set to 375°F (190°C).
2. **Prepare Chicken:** Place chicken breasts in a baking dish, season with garlic powder and pepper.
3. **Add Toppings:** Spread cream cheese over chicken, sprinkle with ranch seasoning, cheddar, and bacon.
4. **Bake:** Cook for 25 minutes until chicken is fully cooked.

Keto Egg Roll in a Bowl

Ingredients:

- 1 lb ground pork or chicken
- ½ head cabbage, shredded
- 1 small carrot, shredded
- 2 cloves garlic, minced
- 2 tbsp soy sauce or coconut aminos
- 1 tsp sesame oil
- 1 tsp grated ginger
- ½ tsp red pepper flakes (optional)

Instructions:

1. **Cook Meat:** Brown ground pork/chicken in a skillet, then remove excess fat.
2. **Add Vegetables:** Stir in garlic, cabbage, carrot, and ginger. Cook until softened.
3. **Season & Serve:** Add soy sauce, sesame oil, and red pepper flakes.

Low-Carb Chicken Parmesan

Ingredients:

- 2 boneless, skinless chicken breasts
- ½ cup almond flour
- ½ cup grated Parmesan cheese
- 1 egg, beaten
- 1 cup sugar-free marinara sauce
- ½ cup shredded mozzarella cheese
- 1 tsp Italian seasoning
- Salt and pepper to taste

Instructions:

1. **Preheat Oven:** Set to 375°F (190°C).
2. **Bread Chicken:** Dip chicken in egg, then coat with almond flour, Parmesan, and Italian seasoning.
3. **Bake:** Place on a baking sheet and bake for 20 minutes.
4. **Add Sauce & Cheese:** Top with marinara sauce and mozzarella, bake for 10 more minutes.

Keto-Friendly Gumbo

Ingredients:

- 1 lb chicken thighs, diced
- ½ lb andouille sausage, sliced
- ½ lb shrimp, peeled and deveined
- 1 small onion, chopped
- ½ bell pepper, chopped
- 2 cloves garlic, minced
- 3 cups chicken broth
- 1 tbsp Cajun seasoning
- ½ tsp smoked paprika
- ½ tsp gumbo file powder
- 1 tbsp butter

Instructions:

1. **Cook Meat:** Sauté chicken and sausage in butter until browned.
2. **Add Vegetables:** Stir in onion, bell pepper, and garlic.
3. **Simmer:** Add broth, Cajun seasoning, and paprika. Simmer for 20 minutes.
4. **Add Shrimp & Finish:** Stir in shrimp and gumbo file powder. Cook for 5 more minutes.

Baked Feta and Tomato Zoodles

Ingredients:

- 1 block feta cheese
- 2 cups cherry tomatoes
- 2 tbsp olive oil
- ½ tsp garlic powder
- ½ tsp dried oregano
- 2 medium zucchinis, spiralized

Instructions:

1. **Preheat Oven:** Set to 400°F (200°C).
2. **Roast Tomatoes & Feta:** Place feta and tomatoes in a baking dish. Drizzle with olive oil and seasonings. Bake for 20 minutes.
3. **Add Zoodles:** Stir in zucchini noodles and mix with roasted feta and tomatoes.
4. **Serve:** Enjoy with fresh basil.

Stuffed Chicken Breast with Cream Cheese and Spinach

Ingredients:

- 2 boneless, skinless chicken breasts
- ½ cup cream cheese
- ½ cup shredded mozzarella cheese
- 1 cup fresh spinach, chopped
- 1 tsp garlic powder
- ½ tsp salt
- ½ tsp black pepper

Instructions:

1. **Preheat Oven:** Set to 375°F (190°C).
2. **Prepare Filling:** Mix cream cheese, mozzarella, spinach, garlic powder, salt, and pepper.
3. **Stuff Chicken:** Cut a pocket into each chicken breast and fill with mixture.
4. **Bake:** Place on a baking sheet and bake for 25 minutes.

Keto Tuna Melt on Cloud Bread

Ingredients:

- **Cloud Bread:**
    - 3 eggs, separated
    - 3 tbsp cream cheese, softened
    - ¼ tsp cream of tartar
    - ½ tsp salt
- **Tuna Melt Filling:**
    - 1 can tuna, drained
    - 2 tbsp mayonnaise
    - ¼ cup shredded cheddar cheese
    - 1 tsp Dijon mustard
    - ½ tsp garlic powder
    - Salt and pepper to taste

Instructions:

1. **Make Cloud Bread:**
    - Preheat oven to 300°F (150°C).
    - Beat egg whites with cream of tartar until stiff peaks form.
    - In another bowl, mix egg yolks, cream cheese, and salt. Gently fold into egg whites.
    - Spoon onto a baking sheet and bake for 20 minutes.
2. **Prepare Tuna Mixture:** Mix all filling ingredients.
3. **Assemble & Melt:** Spread tuna mixture on cloud bread, top with cheese, and broil until melted.

Garlic Butter Baked Cod

Ingredients:

- 2 cod fillets
- 3 tbsp butter, melted
- 2 cloves garlic, minced
- 1 tbsp lemon juice
- ½ tsp salt
- ¼ tsp black pepper
- 1 tsp fresh parsley, chopped

Instructions:

1. **Preheat Oven:** Set to 400°F (200°C).
2. **Prepare Cod:** Place cod fillets in a baking dish.
3. **Make Garlic Butter:** Mix butter, garlic, lemon juice, salt, and pepper. Pour over cod.
4. **Bake:** Cook for 12-15 minutes. Garnish with parsley before serving.

Keto Greek Meatballs with Tzatziki Sauce

Ingredients:

- **Meatballs:**
    - 1 lb ground beef or lamb
    - ½ cup almond flour
    - ½ tsp garlic powder
    - ½ tsp onion powder
    - 1 tsp oregano
    - 1 egg
    - ½ tsp salt
- **Tzatziki Sauce:**
    - ½ cup Greek yogurt
    - ½ cucumber, grated and squeezed dry
    - 1 clove garlic, minced
    - 1 tbsp lemon juice
    - 1 tsp dill
    - Salt and pepper to taste

Instructions:

1. **Preheat Oven:** Set to 375°F (190°C).
2. **Make Meatballs:** Mix all ingredients, form into balls, and bake for 20 minutes.
3. **Prepare Tzatziki:** Mix all sauce ingredients and chill.
4. **Serve:** Enjoy meatballs with tzatziki sauce.

Keto Fried Chicken (Almond Flour Breading)

Ingredients:

- 2 boneless, skinless chicken breasts
- 1 cup almond flour
- ½ cup grated Parmesan cheese
- 1 egg, beaten
- ½ tsp garlic powder
- ½ tsp paprika
- ½ tsp salt
- ¼ tsp black pepper
- ½ cup oil for frying

Instructions:

1. **Prepare Chicken:** Slice chicken into strips.
2. **Coat Chicken:** Dip in egg, then coat with almond flour, Parmesan, and seasonings.
3. **Fry:** Heat oil in a skillet and fry chicken for 3-4 minutes per side until golden.
4. **Serve:** Enjoy with sugar-free dipping sauce.

Keto Zuppa Toscana Soup

Ingredients:

- ½ lb Italian sausage
- ½ head cauliflower, chopped
- 2 cups kale, chopped
- 3 cups chicken broth
- ½ cup heavy cream
- 2 cloves garlic, minced
- ½ tsp red pepper flakes
- 1 tbsp butter

Instructions:

1. **Cook Sausage:** Brown sausage in butter, then set aside.
2. **Simmer Broth:** Add garlic, broth, and cauliflower. Simmer until tender.
3. **Add Cream & Kale:** Stir in heavy cream, kale, and red pepper flakes. Cook for 5 minutes.
4. **Serve:** Enjoy warm.

Keto Bacon-Wrapped Meatballs

Ingredients:

- 1 lb ground beef
- ½ cup shredded cheese
- 1 tsp garlic powder
- ½ tsp salt
- ½ tsp black pepper
- 4 slices bacon, cut in half

Instructions:

1. **Preheat Oven:** Set to 375°F (190°C).
2. **Make Meatballs:** Mix beef, cheese, garlic powder, salt, and pepper. Shape into balls.
3. **Wrap with Bacon:** Wrap each meatball with bacon and secure with a toothpick.
4. **Bake:** Cook for 20-25 minutes.

Spinach and Cheese Stuffed Mushrooms

Ingredients:

- 10 large mushrooms, stems removed
- 1 cup spinach, chopped
- ½ cup cream cheese
- ¼ cup shredded mozzarella
- 1 clove garlic, minced
- ½ tsp salt

Instructions:

1. **Preheat Oven:** Set to 375°F (190°C).
2. **Make Filling:** Sauté spinach and garlic, then mix with cream cheese, mozzarella, and salt.
3. **Stuff Mushrooms:** Fill mushrooms with mixture.
4. **Bake:** Cook for 15-20 minutes.